Lunch
Bag
Notes

Lunch Bag Notes

Ann Marie Parisi
& Al Parisi

Everyday Advice
from a Dad
to His Daughter

LOYOLAPRESS.

CHICAGO

LOYOLAPRESS.

3441 N. ASHLAND AVENUE
CHICAGO, ILLINOIS 60657
(800) 621-1008
WWW.LOYOLABOOKS.ORG

An earlier edition of *Lunch Bag Notes* was self-published by the authors under the Trafford Publishing imprint.

Cover and interior design by Adam Moroschan

Library of Congress Cataloging-in-Publication Data
Parisi, Al.
  Lunch bag notes : everyday advice from a dad to his daughter / Al Parisi &
Ann Marie Parisi.
      p. cm.
  ISBN 0-8294-2060-6
  1. Fathers—Religious life. 2. Fathers and daughters—Religious aspects—
Christianity. 3. Christian life. 4. Conduct of life. I. Parisi, Ann Marie. II. Title.
BV4846.P35 2004
248.8'33—dc22

                                                    2004006760

Printed in Canada
04 05 06 07 08 Webcom 10 9 8 7 6 5 4 3 2 1

We dedicate this book to each other,
as a sign of our mutual love and support.

Introduction

The Parisi family is a normal, well-adjusted, first-generation Italian American family. My mom, Mary, and my dad, Al, both grew up in Brooklyn, New York, in an Italian-American community called Bensonhurst. My dad was instructed in his faith by his mom (my grandmother) and an elderly babysitter. From an early age he felt a calling to the priesthood, and he was encouraged to pursue this calling by the parish priests whom he served. He was the weekend sacristan, a weekday guy Friday, the school janitor, a basketball coach, the Junior Holy Name Society president, and a member of the teen club. He was an A student, was the class comedian, read voraciously, and was a great raconteur. As early as the sixth grade, Dad developed a penchant for writing short stories for his classmates.

Through their middle-school years, Dad, along with his lifelong best friend, Alan, and Alan's dad, would walk over a mile, at least twice monthly, to the nearest public library. They returned the four books they had borrowed on their previous visit and, as usual, argued with the librarian about the four-book limit. Dad enjoyed reading everything from sports biographies to Hardy Boys mysteries. As he got older, he added the classics and motivational books to his reading list. Today, he has an interesting library in his office. One bookcase contains various Bibles, books on Catholicism and motivational books by Steven R. Covey, Les Brown, NBA Coach Pat Riley, former Notre Dame football coach Lou Holtz, and others. Another bookcase is dedicated to "his" New York Yankees, especially Mickey Mantle, his childhood sports idol. Instead of sitting in traffic and complaining during his commute to work, my dad would listen to books on tape, most of which were religious or motivational.

Dad credits much of his success to having been well-read, but he never fails to mention the excellent mentors he had in his life and his inner drive to make his parents proud of him. He says there was one specific incident in his teen life that was so poignant it still seems like it happened to him only yesterday. One evening on a hot and sticky summer night in Brooklyn, New York, many of the neighbors and their kids were sitting on the steps or on chaise lounges in front of Dad's house. As Jack's Ice Cream and Candy Truck made its usual stop in front of the house, all the kids ran to their parents for money to buy an ice cream or cold drink. Dad ran to his pop and asked him for ten cents for a Sunny Boy. My grandfather was engaged in conversation with a neighbor and seemingly ignored my dad. Dad kept tugging at Grandfather's shirt, repeatedly asking for a dime. My dad was ready to give up, but then a minor miracle happened: the neighbor to whom my grandfather was talking reached into his pocket and handed Dad a dime. Dad dashed to the truck and got his drink.

Later that evening when everyone returned to their homes, Dad had a big surprise coming. His dad punished him severely because my dad had embarrassed my grandfather in public. My grandfather did not have any money to give my dad; that's why he was ignoring Dad, though Dad of course hadn't figured it out. "What a lesson I learned that night. It never occurred to me that we were poor. I promised myself someday I would buy my parents a home." It was a promise that he would later keep.

Occasionally, girls in my dad's classes would ask him to write love letters for them. He was the Cyrano de Bergerac of his day. The letters must have been good because about three years ago I had the pleasure of overhearing a conversation between Dad and a couple for whom he had performed his literary magic. I knew of the couple and Dad's role in bringing them together from his recitation of their story. The funny thing was that until that conversation, the husband never knew what my dad had done. When the cat was let out of the bag, the three of them laughed so loud I'm sure you could have heard it across the continent. I share this to show that even as a teen my dad was industrious, confident, and highly motivated. I am told he was a leader by example, and that peers and even older folks turned to him for advice and counsel. Nothing has changed since then; today, he's all that he was then, and more.

My parents went to rival high schools (New Utrecht and Lafayette), but late in the summer of 1973 they met, and it was love at first sight. It wasn't until March of 1974, however, that they went on their first date.

Both sets of my grandparents were old-fashioned, but my maternal grandparents were especially so. They were delighted to meet Mary's "friend," particularly, or perhaps only, because he spoke fluent Italian, was from the neighborhood, and had a big car. This last point was particularly important because my grandparents didn't own a car, nor did they even have drivers' licenses. My dad quickly became part of the family. He became the family chauffeur and "gofer," and then my Uncle Joey's tutor (Joey was twelve years old at that time).

My grandparents came to rely on him for many other things, like help in installing windows, walls, and ceilings, and in wine-making. After about seven months, my dad felt it was time to "pop the question"—no, not a marriage proposal, but an asking-my-mom-for-a-first-date proposal to the annual parish sports dinner dance. The dance was scheduled for Saturday, March 22, 1974, and would be attended by the priests and nuns of the parish. My dad was also part of the post-dance cleanup committee, since the auditorium served not only as a basketball arena Monday through Friday but was also used to handle the overflow crowds during Sunday Mass.

When Dad asked Mom to the dance, she said there was no way her parents would let her go out on a date. A bit over-confident, my dad said, "They'll never say no to me." He couldn't have been more wrong: request denied. My dad was terribly hurt, but he hung in there. He engaged his parents, the parish priests, the Blessed Mother, and his favorite saints. Against all odds, my grandfather finally relented, and a romance was begun. After that first date, my dad and mom dated several times a week for four years. Their dates usually consisted of sitting around the table in my grandparents' kitchen and watching TV. On rare occasions, my mom and dad were allowed to leave the premises and visit relatives. This story of my parents' dating is an example of the character and deter-mination my dad had early in life.

Out of the need to support his family and to prepare for his upcoming marriage, my dad attended Brooklyn College at night while working full-time in the banking industry during the day. He graduated cum laude in four and a half years, and somehow also had the time to reestablish a chapter of his beloved fraternity, Alpha Phi Delta, on campus. He married Mom on July 29, 1978. He was twenty-three on their wedding day; Mom turned twenty-one during their honeymoon in Italy. Despite Dad's young age, he was appointed branch manager of the local savings and loan.

I was born in Brooklyn, New York, on December 11, 1982. Doctors said I was a miracle birth. Not only was I a breach baby, but my umbilical cord also was tied tightly around my neck and shoulders. An emergency C-section apparently saved my life. My parents wasted no time in getting me baptized. They thanked the Blessed Virgin Mary with a nice gift to the church, and named me after her and her mother, St. Ann. I was the first grandchild to both sets of grandparents, and I'm told that they naturally doted on me. It was with heavy hearts that, three months later, my parents had to inform my grandparents that Dad had accepted a promotion, and my parents and I were moving to Columbus, Ohio.

A year later, Dad was given the responsibility of starting a new division of his company and was transferred back to New York City. My grandparents were thrilled. Then eleven months later, Dad received the proverbial "offer you can't refuse," and Mom, Dad and I moved out to Southern California. Mom continued to stay at home, and we did everything together. It was a real bonding experience. Since we had no family in California, I went everywhere with my parents, including fancy restaurants and hotels. I guess I was well-behaved enough that Mom and

Dad were able to take me along without any anxiety; people we met often doted on me just like my grandparents had. I can remember both Mom and Dad teaching me manners and prayers. They slowly introduced me to the Catholic faith.

Mom encouraged my involvement in several activities at a young age, including music, dancing, and, of course, acting—after all, we were living near Hollywood. I attended Agoura Hills (a Los Angeles suburb) schools and continued studying voice, piano, and dancing, and even acted in a local play with Angela, one my closest friends. My dad tried pushing me to play a sport, so I gave softball a try . . . to this day I see myself running the bases backwards. It was a short and failed endeavor.

At the top of Dad's list of priorities was the religious education of my brother Anthony and me. Dad took the responsibility seriously. He didn't leave the job for some teacher to do in the future. He taught us by reading to us about the church and the saints. He gave us rosary beads and religious cards. Mostly, however, he taught us by his own pious example. As a result, I learned my faith. [Today, like Dad, I teach religious education. At the time I am writing this, I am a junior in college and I aspire to teach some day at a Catholic school, hopefully at my home parish.]

Success continued to follow my dad throughout his career; he eventually became the chairman of the board and CEO of Acqua Group, Inc., a national drinking-water company that he founded and took public in 1990.

My dad's faith and his understanding of stewardship remained vitally important to him throughout these good times. He was always humble and often embarrassed by his success. He even kept his well-deserved Mercedes in the garage so his friends wouldn't assume he had changed. He attended weekday Mass as often as he could and almost never missed first Friday or first Saturday. He became a Eucharistic Minister, lector, religious education teacher, and confirmation leader. He volunteered or was sought out to join church, sports, and civic organizations. When a group of boys needed a coach, the league approached my dad, even though my brother was still too young to play himself. Not only did Dad coach the team, he also volunteered to be a league director. He has been Anthony's hero, always there for him, whether it is for school or church-related activities, sports, or just hanging with him.

In 1994, my father's true mettle was tested, as he puts it. After suffering indescribable headaches for months, doctors diagnosed him with a malignant brain tumor. Thanks to the prayers of many friends—some of whom my father claims hadn't prayed in years—neighbors, relatives, and parishioners, and the hands of a skillful world-famous surgeon, Dad survived the very scary operation to remove the tumor. Though the operation was successful, after this ordeal, the doctors decided that Dad should receive six weeks of daily, one-hour doses of radiation to make certain every last malignant cell was eradicated from his body. Mom and Dad quickly arranged for Anthony and me to go on a "vacation" to Brooklyn, New York, to shield us from the trauma that was about to unfold.

Being separated from your parents at such a youthful age is difficult enough, but when it's due to your parent's serious illness, it is unbelievably hard. Knowing our dad was suffering while Anthony and I were being entertained tore us apart. *Is Dad going to be okay? Is he going to die?* These were the types of questions that we asked ourselves every day. He was always on our minds, and we prayed for him daily. I felt so guilty not being home for him. I couldn't wait to see him again and give him a tight, tight hug. *That will make him feel better,* I thought.

Mom described Dad's days during his radiation treatment as awful. He was unable to eat or sleep, was blurry-eyed and unable to read or watch TV, and was constantly sick to his stomach. Mom said there were days she literally had to drag him off the sofa and into the car. As she drove him to UCLA for his treatments, she had to stuff crackers in his mouth to keep him from vomiting.

Finally, Dad's radiation treatment ended, and Anthony and I returned home. Incidentally, that "vacation" was the first time Anthony and I were ever separated from both our parents. I grew up a lot on that trip.

Doctors instructed my dad to take ten to eleven months off from work so his body and brain could heal. Unfortunately, Dad's pride—his *Sicilian pride,* as he likes to say—made him believe he could go back to work after just six weeks. By going back to work so early he exacerbated the collateral damage caused by the postoperative radiation. About a year later, Dad found himself totally incapable of working as an executive. He suffered, and continues to suffer, from chronic and acute back, shoulder, and neck pain; loss of short-term memory, 100 percent loss of hearing in his right ear; loss of balance; and frequent disorientation, just to mention a few of his ailments. Despite all this, he continues to do all he can for others, especially his family and his God.

It wasn't easy for Dad to accept his cross at first. He suffered survivor guilt and wondered why God let him survive and not another gentleman in our community, Mom's obstetrician, who was the same age as Dad and also had a brain tumor. As the familiar and routine life he had led before his cancer collapsed, Dad soon became very depressed. He was no longer a successful businessman and entrepreneur, but was now "Mr. Mom." He stood by helplessly as a restaurant and other business endeavors began to fail. Through it all, Dad never let his faith falter. He credits the newfound opportunity to receive the Holy Eucharist each day as the reason for his will to persevere. He came to view his cross as an opportunity to relieve the suffering of some of the souls in purgatory by offering up his pain for them every day.

Dad eventually accepted the role of stay-at-home dad and redefined this position as CEO of Parisi Enterprises. He regained most of his good humor and positive outlook on life, and returned to writing memos. These memos, however, were far more important than the ones to his subordinates that his secretary would type on his embossed stationery. He wrote his new memos to me and my friends on brown lunch bags. They are the basis for this book.

My friends who read Dad's memos with me are the inspiration behind this book. We all grew up together. We spent our time attending football games, watching our siblings play sports, girl scouting, attending school dances, and going to whatever other local activities we could talk our parents into. We celebrated one another's birthdays with pajama parties and discussed the usual things: fashion, boys, movies, TV shows, school happenings, and so on. Our names are Angela, B. T., Becky, Brynn, Erin, Jenny, Julia, Malia, Marissa, and, of course, Ann Marie (me).

None of us had a sister, which is one reason why we were all so close. We were very much like siblings. We affectionately called ourselves "Al's Gals" because we grew up under my dad's watch. He was our chauffeur, religious education teacher, confirmation leader, and mentor. We could talk to him about anything, and he relished every moment with us.

From kindergarten through high school, Al's Gals spent most weekends at my house. Both my mom and dad were pleased we did so. My mom made us home-baked goodies, hot chocolate, and hot apple cider, but our favorite treat was Martinelli's Gold Medal Sparkling Cider with pizza or my mom's focaccia.

My mom, who was also our school campus supervisor, would occasionally join us and make us laugh hysterically with school anecdotes or tales of her courtship with Dad. We were, however, excellent at entertaining ourselves. We chatted for hours, watched videos, swam, or performed skits, which we would tape and later watch, as we roared with laughter. Malia served as camerawomen (she is now studying photography at California State University, Northridge, and aspires to work in Hollywood someday). Becky, one of the loquacious ones (I was the other), served as our announcer/commentator. Mom and Dad often sat in to watch either our live or taped performances; sometimes they even watched both. It was so cool to see them thoroughly enjoying themselves.

Our parents would frequently get together with or without us girls. We became "family" to one another, as our biological families were scattered throughout the East and Midwest. Because we were very much like sisters, at times there were also heated discussions and sibling rivalries among us. However, we always managed to resolve our differences rather quickly.

Whether in our religious education classes or at our weekend get-togethers, my dad was adept at sharing thinly veiled morality stories with us. What a wonderful storyteller he was and continues to be. We never knew if his stories were truth or fiction, but it didn't matter—they motivated and inspired us. He could read all of us like proverbial books, and always had words of encouragement for each of us individually. He was very aware of our "important" teenage issues and somehow never overstayed his welcome.

One particular morning during the fall semester of our sophomore year at Agoura High School, Dad was inspired to write a few words of encouragement on my brown lunch bag. I discovered it when I sat down to eat. After reading it, it was obvious to me that Dad had overheard Al's Gals engaged in an unusually loud and sometimes mean-spirited debate. He may not have understood the issue exactly, but he was concerned because I went to bed upset that night.

The next day, there was another note written on my brown bag. Just like the day before, I didn't discover it until lunchtime when I took my lunch out of my backpack. And just like the day before, I read it very quickly, crunched it up, and tossed it into the trash. Soon afterwards, I realized Dad's notes were becoming an everyday occurrence. I began to look forward to reading them—I was careful, however, not to let the rest of Al's Gals at the table see the notes, which I thought were too private. The notes were mostly timely thoughts on everyday issues and personal advice for me.

After a while, the hot debate was forgotten, and the Al's Gals lunch table was back to normal. The content of Dad's notes lightened up a bit as he sensed the normalcy among us.

Reading Dad's notes soon became ritualistic and more important to me than the lunch contained in the brown bag. I was no longer discreet. The first thing I would do was empty the contents and then carefully "iron" the bag with my hands. The other Al's Gals began to notice my ritual; they would come over and try to read the notes over my shoulder. I finally came clean and told them what Dad had been doing. They showed genuine interest and excitement, and soon it became a custom for us to pass the hand-ironed lunch bag around the table, so each Al's Gal could read it. Later, friends from our extended group, which included boys, were coming by to read the notes. They knew my dad pretty well, so they were curious.

When I eventually told Dad about his extended audience, he was very moved. He said he enjoyed writing them and, if I liked, he would continue to do so. In fact, motivated by his new readership, Dad began to write in a fashion that had a broader appeal. Dad's notes, though they evolved, were still written all on one side of the brown bag, and they remained simple and profound. Little did I, or any of Al's Gals, realize then that Dad's notes were truly maxims for leading a happy and fulfilling life.

These beautiful, heartwarming messages of love that my friends and I were blessed to read were meant to inspire us to believe in ourselves and to make sound choices in our lives. They were clear and concise, and never preachy. The lunch bags Dad wrote on were purchased at the local Costco Warehouse. They were inexpensive, plain brown-paper bags; the messages written on them, however, were timeless and priceless.

I saved these brown-bag notes, unbeknownst to my dad, to share them with my children some day. I stuffed the bags in a sneaker box and put the box on a shelf in my bedroom closet. About two years ago, as I was cleaning and packing up that closet, the sneaker box fell on my head, and the notes scattered everywhere. When I told my dad what happened and that I'd saved nearly all his notes, he was so touched.

About that time, we had been invited to dinner at a friend's house. The host couple, Elizabeth and Stefan Gaudio, were my dad's childhood friends. Dad couldn't wait to tell them about the notes he wrote, how I had saved them, and, of course, how the box bonked me on my head, and the notes went flying everywhere. We all laughed. Then, after a pause, Elizabeth suggested we *do* something with the notes. *Like what?* we wondered. She explained that the notes could be made into a book. We discussed it a little further, and then somehow over dinner the discussion was dropped. It seemed, though, that everyone with whom Dad shared the story had a similar suggestion.

Eventually, I resumed the discussion with Dad and ultimately decided, with Dad's blessing, to share these notes with other teens and their dads, who often have difficulty expressing their emotions with each other. Knowing nothing about the publishing business, Dad volunteered to get on the Internet and try to learn what he could. Dad has difficulty learning new concepts as a result of the collateral damage he sustained during his radiation treatment. Thankfully, he was at least able to determine that the best and fastest way to have the book published was to self-publish it. I did so through Trafford Publishing, located in Canada. We chose Trafford because they were very professional and very understanding of Dad's limitations. Mary Lucas, our representative, made certain to follow up on every detail and guided us step by step.

The original version of the book was released in the spring of 2003. We promptly began to use the book as a fund-raiser for our parish, St. Jude Roman Catholic Church in Westlake Village, and for a few departments at my alma mater, Agoura High. I started a Lunch Bag Notes Scholarship Fund at Agoura, as well. The scholarship goes to the person who most exemplifies the ideals of *Lunch Bag Notes*. I had the pleasure of awarding the inaugural scholarship this past June to Brooke Hawkins, a well-deserving recipient, who uses her time and talent for the betterment of others.

Word spread throughout the neighboring communities, and articles appeared in all the local papers, as well as our diocesan newspaper. Readers' comments were remarkable and humbling. They came in the form of cards, notes, teary-eyed telephone calls, e-mails, and in person from teenagers, parents, grandparents, educators, and priests. Dad and I knew the notes were touching peoples' lives. At that point, Dad also realized that what he thought were *his* notes were actually inspired by God. In late May 2003—barely six weeks after we had received our first courtesy copies of the book—Dad was confident that the mini–test-marketing we had done was successful. There was interest out there for an inspirational and simple book on how to live a good, moral life. "Perhaps we should have a parallel plan to solicit a Catholic publisher for you to get the book out to as many people as possible," Dad said.

We sent a cover letter, readers' comments, newspaper clippings, and the book to several publishers, and received the standard thanks-but-no-thanks letter from a few of them. Three publishers expressed an interest in acquiring the book. Dad spent many hours e-mailing and updating each of them, but was often frustrated by the absence of return calls or e-mails. It was literally a painful process for Dad, as he suffers chronic and acute back pain, which is exacerbated when he sits too long at the computer, but he was on a proverbial "mission from God."

The first to respond affirmatively that they wanted to purchase the publishing rights to *Lunch Bag Notes* was Loyola Press. This new Loyola Press edition incorporates some wonderful changes suggested by the editorial staff: an expanded introduction, questions for reflection, and space for journaling.

Here is another example of how providential this whole experience has been (remember the box bonking me on the head). Sometime in April 2003, Dad was asked to attend the International Catholic Stewardship Conference in Chicago, Illinois, as a representative of our parish. That was well before we even thought about traditional publishers. Remarkably, Loyola Press is headquartered in Chicago. The conference took place October 5–8, 2003. At the end of the conference, Loyola sent a car to pick up Dad. Upon arrival, there was a sign welcoming him. He met with the entire staff, who, like Trafford's Mary Lucas, treated my dad with dignity and grace.

The notes, unedited except for two minor attributions, follow. I sincerely hope this tiny treasure of Dad's wisdom serves to motivate and inspire you to *believe in yourself and boldly follow your dreams.*

—Ann Marie Parisi

How to Use This Book

Since most of you will find that you have either experienced similar situations to the ones described in the notes or likely will encounter them, each note is accompanied by a journal page with a brief comment to stimulate your thought processes. We recommend you record your feelings and your emotions, or anything else that comes to mind after reading the accompanying note. Usually, your first thoughts will be the strongest and the most meaningful. By taking the time to write out your thoughts, you will be more likely to understand how to apply the note to your own life experience. For instance, you may be conflicted about a decision, choice, or action you need to take. By journaling, you can better assess the situation. Ben Franklin, whenever he was faced with a crucial decision, would write out each possible choice on a separate piece of paper, and then draw a line down the middle of the page. On one side he would write the potential positive outcomes of his decision, and on the other side he would write the potential negative outcomes. After doing so, he would opt for the choice that had the most potential for a positive result. Like most good decision makers, he took his time deciding, but once he did, he was firm in his commitment.

The right-hand pages are lined for your convenience when journaling. At the bottom of each journal page, you will also find the theme(s) of the accompanying note, for easy reference.

Lunch Bag Notes

Dearest Ann Marie,

I understand Al's Gals are going through a difficult time.

Remember you are very blessed with beauty, grace, talent, maturity, and a wonderful home life.

Once in a while, even friends make unkind remarks to each other. You shouldn't, however, let these remarks get you too far down in the dumps. Most often, these words are spoken out of frustration, jealousy, and anger. They are <u>not</u> a true reflection of you. You see it is far easier to bring others (you) down than it is to rise up to their (your) level.

Love, Dad

Do you ever put down your friends or make mean comments about others? How do you think this makes them feel? When others offend and hurt you, do you react hastily, and inflame the situation? Anger is natural in these situations, but the mature person pauses, says a quick silent pray, and responds charitably. Friendships are worth saving, wouldn't you agree?

{ **Friendship, Attitude** }

Dearest Ann Marie,

Each of us has time, talent, and treasure to share with our fellow man.

I urge you to exploit your talents lest they shrivel away, to offer your time to charitable and civic causes, and some day to share your treasure with those less fortunate than you.

Love, Dad

Remember: **All we own is on loan from God.** We are only stewards of his gifts. He expects us to take good care of his gifts and to share them with members of our community. Do you feel good about the way you're currently sharing God's gifts? If not, how can you share your gifts with others?

{ Stewardship }

Dearest Ann Marie,

One of the nicest things we can do for someone is to simply listen to him or her and show genuine concern. So many people listen with their own "agenda," as if to say, "I have something more important to say than whatever you're saying."

Listening should be raised to an art form. It is a challenging but necessary component of "dialogue." The first two letters of the word—di—mean two. How can we dialogue if we don't care to listen to others?

Love, Dad

Aren't you annoyed when you are ignored or when no one shows an interest in what you are saying? Think about that the next time you have the urge to interrupt someone else. How can you be a better listener?

{ **Friendship, Happiness** }

Dearest Ann Marie,

You may be shocked to hear this, but I urge you to never grow up. Be like Peter Pan.

What I mean, of course, is to appreciate life like a child getting his or her first bicycle or a child visiting Disneyland. The unconditional love and innocence we had as children is the antidote to many of society's ills—prejudice, hatred, selfishness, etc.

As you have heard me say many times, your attitude is all-important. Attitude pretty much determines how much you can grow as an individual. Use this acronym to constantly remind yourself to maintain a positive attitude—<u>S</u>uperior <u>M</u>ental <u>A</u>ttitude <u>R</u>esults in <u>T</u>riumph!

Be SMART!

Love, Dad

Are you rushing to grow up and passing on the joys of youth? If so, you're squandering a wonderful gift God has given you. You'll have plenty of years of adulthood, so slow down and smell the roses. What can you do today to recapture the joy of childhood?

{ Attitude }

Dearest Ann Marie,

There is a saying from Confucius that is very apropos: "I hear and I forget. I see and I remember. I do and I understand."

In other words, it is in the "doing" that we appreciate and learn the meaning of an action or activity, not in thinking or daydreaming about it.

I urge you to use and share your talents and perhaps you will discover why God blessed you with them.

Love, Dad

Do you daydream often about the things you would like to do? If you can "dream," you can "do." One method used by very successful people is to write down your goals with a timetable and a plan for achieving them. What are your goals? What is your plan to achieve them? Post your goals prominently and read them daily.

{ **Attitude, Stewardship** }

Dearest Ann Marie,

A follow-up to yesterday's Chinese saying: A Roman proverb says, "Fortune favors the bold."

In other words, success is more likely to be achieved by those who recognize and _boldly_ accept life's opportunities.

Roman generals used to "burn the bridges" behind them so their soldiers couldn't retreat. They would have to forge ahead, regardless of the obstacles. The analogy, Ann Marie, is to not let peer pressure or other hindrances stop you.

Love, Dad

Are your friends or anyone else holding you back from fulfilling your dreams? Perhaps in the future you should share your plans only with those who are supportive. Go back and read the advice given after the first lunch note. Who is supportive of your dreams? Who isn't?

{ Attitude, Friendship }

Dearest Ann Marie,

The decisions we make every day have a profound impact on where we are in life, both spiritually and physically.

Often, these decisions are the "safe choices" because, as Aristotle, the Greek philosopher, said, "Man perpetuates the familiar." Rarely do people choose to venture beyond their comfort zone and challenge themselves. To paraphrase Henry David Thoreau, they live lives of quiet desperation.

I encourage you and all of Al's Gals to "boldly go where no man/woman has gone before."

Love, Dad

Do you find yourself in a rut? If so, determine why, and self-correct. Usually, all it takes is to *do* something. The hardest part is the first step. Decide to be proactive. God wants us to be joyful. What has given you joy in your life? What can you do that is joyful? Get up and do it again, or stretch yourself and try something new.

{ Choices, Attitude }

Dearest Ann Marie,

St. Francis of Assisi, wary of conventional wisdom and aristocratic duties, renounced his wealth, inheritance, and power. He adopted a much simpler life by living in the forest in abject poverty, yet he was joyful. He danced, told humorous stories, and laughed. He learned to appreciate the beauty of nature and acquired inner peace.

The lesson to us is a reminder to slow the pace and learn to "smell the roses," to take a break from the hustle and bustle of life and appreciate the gift of life.

Love, Dad

Give yourself a break; it is possible that no one else will. You need to recharge your batteries, too. Fatigue is often the cause of hasty decisions and accidents. What is causing undue stress in your life? Do you find yourself exhausted from too many activities? Has being too busy or too tired caused you to make any bad decisions? What can you do to relieve some of this stress?

Take the time to have a "coffee break" with God daily. St. Francis's example of serenity is proof that happiness isn't dependent on *things*.

{ Attitude, Stress }

Dearest Ann Marie,

Make today a great day by living it to the max!

Carpe diem!

Love, Dad

The Marine motto "carpe diem" is Latin for "seize the day." Do you know every day is full of opportunity to improve yourself physically, mentally, and spiritually? What can you do to seize the day?

Exercise your body, mind, and spirit. How will you start today? Write down your commitment; that's why the lines are there.

{ Attitude }

To Ann Marie, our angel,

Happiness is enjoying what you have and what's around you at every moment. . . . Treasure today because it's the "present."

Love you 4-ever, Mom substituting for Dad

What material things make you happy? Why? Reexamine your priorities. What else that you can't buy in a store makes you happy? Remember the lessons of St. Francis.

{ Happiness }

Dearest Ann Marie,

You feel as you think. If you think positively, you'll feel good. On the other hand, if you raise doubts about yourself, you will feel bad. It's that simple.

When a bad feeling comes over you, talk yourself out of it by reflecting on all the gifts and graces God has given you. Frequently remind yourself how much you are loved, and fill your mind throughout the day with positive affirmations. One of my favorites is: I am getting better each and every day.

Love, Dad

Do you have negative thoughts, doubts about your-self, or inhibitions? Why? What can you do to change your outlook? Try something new; face a fear. Raise your hand in class; be bold and smile.

We train children by repetition; you can still do the same thing to yourself. Empty your mind of negativity and fill it with positive affirmations. What are five great things about you?

{ Attitude }

Dearest Ann Marie,

Computers can be a good metaphor for life. For instance, whenever we put inaccurate data in a computer, it spits out incorrect results. However, when we input accurate data in a computer, it spits out accurate results.

We are much the same way. If we fill our minds, bodies, and souls with goodness, then we in turn will be good, won't we?

Love, Dad

By now, you are probably on your way to having a positive attitude every day. If not, have you been going it alone? Is there anyone who can help you to maintain a positive attitude during the day? Try starting each morning this way: When you awake, before getting out of bed, say "Good Morning, Lord. Together let's make it a great day." Now you have a partner. Be bold and be loud, and start tomorrow!

{ Attitude }

Dearest Ann Marie,

It was wonderful to see you smiling and laughing. It was contagious. Glad to say Mom and I both caught it.

Love, Dad

Aren't you more attracted to people who smile than to those who frown?

Doctors say laughing is very therapeutic and good medicine. What is your daily dosage? What can you do to put smiles on others' faces?

{ Attitude }

Dearest Ann Marie,

The Lord said, "I am the way, and the truth, and the life" (John 14:6). That is why we wear a WWJD [What Would Jesus Do? or Walk With Jesus Daily] bracelet. It reminds us to walk with him daily and do as he would do.

It's a simple plan to follow and yet a profound way to lead others.

Love, Dad

Be SMART!

Do you think it's easy or difficult to walk with Jesus daily? Why? Either way, you are right. And either way, he walks with you. When was Jesus with you today? Acknowledge his presence and it will get easier and become habit forming—a good addiction to have.

{ Faith }

Dearest Ann Marie,

I love the words of the song "Don't Worry, Be Happy."

It is a profound message. It means there is no reason to worry about the past, as the past is history. There is no reason to worry about problems we can resolve—just resolve them. There is no reason to worry about things we can't resolve either. The challenge here is to pray for acceptance and deal with the situation appropriately, while accepting God's will.

Love, Dad

What do you worry about? The Boy Scout motto is "Be prepared." Being prepared and doing the right thing is often enough to eliminate needless worry. As an example, if you have studied well and are prepared for a test, you *will do well*, so there is nothing to worry about, is there? Similarly, if you have prepared by doing the right things, then you don't even have to worry about going to heaven, do you? What can you do to reduce your worries?

{ Stress }

Dearest Ann Marie,

Heaven is our ultimate goal. Therefore, each decision we make should take us closer to heaven. It would be the worst of losses to lose sight of this goal, even if it were for only a second.

Remember: WWJD.

Love, Dad

What decisions have you made that took you closer to heaven? When have you lost sight of this goal? Could you imagine anything better than heaven? Of course not; so leave nothing to chance.

{ **Character, Choices** }

Dearest Ann Marie,

In this week of exams, remember to be prepared—study well. In doing so, you will relieve your anxiety and perform well.

As always, pray that you prepare well, and not necessarily for an A.

Love, Dad

Do you pray for an A and then not study well, yet still expect an A? That's like a boxer who blesses himself when he enters the ring expecting to win even though he hasn't trained and prepared well. Ridiculous, isn't it? When have you failed to prepare but still expected an A?

{ Prayer, Stress }

Dearest Ann Marie,

My favorite daily affirmation should serve you well this week:

I believe I am divinely inspired. I believe I will always take the right turn of the road. I believe God will always make a way where there is no way.

Be SMART!

Love, Dad

Affirmations are fuel for your mind. Make up your own as an exercise and write them down. You can also use simple prayers, like "Jesus, help me" or "Holy Spirit, help me," if you aren't sure what to say.

Use this technique throughout the day. It will keep your mind and your soul at peak efficiency.

{ **Prayer** }

Dearest Ann Marie,

Patience is a virtue. Listening to others without an agenda of our own is also a virtue.

Practice these virtues every day. As you grow older, you will better understand their significance.

Love, Dad

Don't you feel great when someone really shows interest in you? Don't you love it when you are not at your best, but people still have patience with you? Don't you really love getting an "atta girl/boy"? Well then, remember to *do unto others as you would have them do unto you* (Matthew 7:12, Luke 6:31).

{ **Character** }

Dearest Ann Marie,

Remember, our moods are created by our thoughts. Peter Pan had it right when he said, "Think happy thoughts."

Tomorrow when you wake up, decide to be happy. You'll be surprised by the results. The mind is like a powerful energy field. Make it produce positive energy for you. Think how happy you are when you sing. The goodness you feel is the result of the "doing."

Love, Dad

When a negative thought comes to mind, quickly think of a happy thought or, better yet, call on the Lord—he's always at your side.

Reminder: When you wake up in the morning, acknowledge the Lord, your partner in the day's activities.

{ **Attitude, Prayer** }

Dearest Ann Marie,

There is nothing that can come your way that God and you can't handle!

Be SMART!

Love, Dad

Recall the affirmation: *I believe I am divinely inspired. I believe I will always take the right turn of the road. I believe God will always make a way where there is no way.*

Where in your life do you need God to make a way?

_____

_____

_____

_____

_____

_____

_____

_____

_____

_____

_____

_____

_____

_____

{ Faith }

Dearest Ann Marie,

Not every day goes as smoothly as we would like. In the midst of dis—appointments, hurts, and difficulties, it is best to take a time—out and ask God to give us the wisdom and fortitude necessary to cope and to make wise choices.

No one may "give you a break today," so give yourself one and talk to God. Oh, and don't forget to listen.

Love, Dad

What disappointments have you experienced? Do you *respond* to the situation in consultation with Jesus or do you *react* on your own? Remember: We react based on our emotions, but we respond based on reason. What difficulties are you facing that Jesus can help you with?

{ Failure }

Dearest Ann Marie,

What would you do if you knew you had only one month left on Earth?

Who would you see?
Who would you call?
What would you try?
Where would you go?

The answers to these questions remind you what elements in your life you should never take for granted.

Imagine how wonderful the world would be if people felt, "This may be the last time I see this person."

Love, Dad

What are your priorities? Write them down and evaluate them. If you had one month to live, what would you do? If necessary, make changes in your life to do those things now.

Dearest Ann Marie,

What an outpouring of love from your friends Friday night. As always, Al's Gals are forever welcome in our home.

Everyone who knows you knows about your compassion and love for others. Yet no one is surprised or amazed. After all, that is what we have come to expect from you.

May God reward you many fold for all your kindnesses.

Thank you for blessing us.

Love, Dad

Who are your friends? Are they supportive or are they a negative influence in your life? Are you supportive of them? What could you do to be a positive influence in their lives?

{ Friendship }

Dearest Ann Marie,

What a fabulous "Sweet Sixteen" weekend.
There is an old adage that says, "We
are judged by the company we keep,"
and another that says, "Show me your
friends and I'll tell you what you are."

Based on my observations this weekend,
you are certainly judged well.

Love, the man who paid for it all, Dad

Another reminder to monitor the company you keep. What do your friends say about who you are? Have others judged you because of your friends? How?

Dearest Ann Marie,

I'm glad you started an exercise regimen.
As you know, exercise produces endorphins,
which will give you that "natural high."
You will get in great shape and your
self—esteem will go up . . . a priceless
gift to yourself.

You inspire me, and I might just join you.

Love, Dad

We need to have a healthy body, mind, and soul in order to be a complete person. Remember, we are made in God's image, but it's up to you to maintain your body. Are you taking care of your body? What can you do to be healthier?

{ **Happiness** }

Dearest Ann Marie,

President Calvin Coolidge once said, "Persistence and determination alone are omnipotent."

In other words, when we set out to accomplish a task:

1. Do it with all the gusto you can muster.
2. Persevere through adversity.
3. Determine that you will invest in yourself to the point of sacrifice.
4. Do not be discouraged by a misstep or two, or even by those who would rather see you fail.

Be SMART!

Love, Dad

Anything worth achieving is worth the effort. Effort is the means to the end. Resolve to make President Coolidge's saying a guidepost in your life. What do you want to accomplish?

{ Attitude }

Dearest Ann Marie,

A real woman is: unselfish, thoughtful, and kind; honest, faithful, and trustworthy; patient, sincere, and forgiving; modest, pure, and chaste; compassionate, caring, and giving.

A great woman: understands chastity, values her sexuality, controls her passion and desires, and knows her body is the temple of the Holy Spirit.

Love, Dad

How many of these qualities can you claim? These qualities cannot be "taught." You must endeavor to develop them on your own. As you begin to claim more and more of these qualities, your self-worth will skyrocket.

In case you were wondering, guys, the same applies to you.

{ **Character** }

Dearest Ann Marie,

You are <u>what</u> and <u>where</u> you are because of the choices you have made in life.

Choices really matter. Every day we choose what to eat, what to wear, what to do, where to go, and with whom to hang out. Each decision, small or big, has an impact, either positive or negative, on others, as well as on us.

The simplest ways to ensure you are making good choices: WWJD and the Golden Rule. Remember.

Love, Dad

What decisions have you made that have had positive results? What decisions have had negative results? Do you make decisions in haste or react emotionally? One characteristic of good decision makers and successful people is to avoid hasty or emotional decisions. Take your time in deciding, evaluate the pluses or minuses of a particular choice, and then be resolute in your decision.

{ Choices }

Dearest Ann Marie,

You have grown up to be such a fine lady.

Thank you for being thoughtful enough to make lunch for me and Anthony, and for helping Anthony study.

Without Mom and I having trust in you, we would not have been able to attend tonight's affair.

We love you so much and always will be your number one fans.

Love, Dad

What responsibilities have your parents given you? Are you trustworthy? Trust is one of the most important components of character. What can you do to gain the trust of others?

{ Character }

Dearest Ann Marie,

It takes a lot of positive inputs to offset a negative input.

Fill your mind and body and soul with positive "stuff," i.e., positive music, positive books, positive movies, positive food, positive thoughts, positive ideas, positive choices and decisions, positive outfits, positive poise, positive self—esteem and confidence, and positive friends. Then you will be able to reach your goals.

Love, Dad

ith what "stuff" are you filling your mind, body, and soul? Are you making a concerted effort to fill yourself and your life with positive things?

Dearest Ann Marie,

The only thing constant in life, ironically, is change.

Change can be exhilarating or excruciating. It all depends on our attitude. If you look forward to change and the new opportunities it brings, it can be very exciting and adventurous.

Remember, attitude is all—important in dictating the outcome of any endeavor.

Love, Dad

What changes have there been in your life? Did you have a positive or a negative attitude toward these changes? Did your attitude affect how you dealt with these changes? How? When it comes to how you react to change, the choice is yours, isn't it?

{ **Attitude** }

Dearest Ann Marie,

Because of our humanity, we sometimes fail. That is why they put erasers on pencils.

We fail when we neglect to do what we should have done or we do what we should not have done.

Regardless, God forgives us and encourages us to try again with more fervor. Even if we fail one thousand times, God will forgive us if we are truly sorry and promise to try again. The Lord asks for progress, not perfection.

Love, Dad

When have you failed? What did you learn from your failure? Did you make progress the next time you tried? Never give up, whether it's a school project, a personal goal, or your relationship with the Lord that is failing. Failure is often the gateway to success.

{ **Failure** }

Dearest Ann Marie,

Friends leave their marks on the world by the love they share with others. In turn, those "others" share their love, and so on and so on. If everyone bought into this concept, what a better world we'd live in.

A beautiful thing about friendship is that it's the gift that keeps on giving. I know of no other teen who values her friendships like you do.

Love, Dad

To whom do you offer your gift of friendship? Are you only friends with people who can "do something" for you? True friendship, like true love, must be unconditional. Which of your friends can do nothing for you, yet are still your friends? If you don't have any friends like this, try befriending someone who can do nothing for you.

{ Friendship }

Dearest Ann Marie,

With the Christmas season quickly approaching, I thought to remind you that the reason for the season is Jesus, not Santa.

We give gifts as an expression of our love for others, much like the Magi did for the infant Jesus more than two thousand years ago.

The greatest gift you can give me is your presence, not your presents.

Love, Dad

How often do you share your time with others? Who have you shared your time with lately? Do you run in a pack or are you a loner? Even though we all need time alone, we also need the company of others. For Christmas this year, or for any other holiday or occasion, give a lonely person you know a present: your presence.

{ **Faith, Stewardship** }

Dearest Ann Marie,

I so much enjoy our weekly confirmation preparedness meetings. The coziness of our living room and the closeness of the group are fantastic. I especially enjoy when your Jewish friends join us, particularly since so much of our curriculum is based on the Hebrew Scriptures.

Their input about their bar mitzvah experiences is enlightening, isn't it?

You are blessed with wonderful friends, Ann Marie.

Love, Dad

Can you objectively say, "I have wonderful friends"? Are some of your friends more wonderful—and say better things about what you are—than others? Why?

{ Friendship }

Dearest Ann Marie,

I truly enjoy our annual family tradition of decorating the house for Christmas during the Thanksgiving weekend, though you and I know it couldn't happen without the two of us. Anthony is too young to remain focused and Mom is too _____ (you fill in the blank).

It is so much fun, isn't it? I enjoy it so much when you show off our work to your friends. I feel pride, as I am sure you do, each time a passerby stops to get a good look.

I hope we will continue this tradition even after you are married.

Love, Dad

What projects do you enjoy doing with your family? Other than spending time with our Lord, there is no more important use of our time. What are some family projects that you can recommend, even if you may have to insist that everyone participate? It may be the boldest thing you do . . . but "just do it." You'll be amazed at the fun you'll have, and the difference it will make.

{ Family }

Dearest Ann Marie,

Don't you enjoy all the holiday movies? Like fine wine, they never get old. The message of hope and trust is awe inspiring, don't you think? Whether it is <u>Rudolph, the Red Nosed Reindeer</u>, <u>March of the Wooden Soldiers</u>, or <u>A Christmas Story</u>, the message is so clear—faith, hope, and charity abide. The other great similarity in these movies is that they all share the message of trust in our fellow man.

To all Al's Gals, may the beauty, the grace, and the spirit of the season be with you throughout the year.

Love, Dad

The Lord wants us to be joyful people. What can you do to share the joy of the holidays with others? What can you do to share the beauty, grace, and love of the season all year long?

{ **Faith, Happiness** }

Dearest Ann Marie,

Remember "Footprints." When times are difficult, as they are now, the Lord carries us through each trial and tribulation. Imagine if we had only ourselves to rely on. How frightening would life be?

But as it is, we are blessed by a loving and caring God.

Love, Dad

Have you ever felt abandoned by friends and family, and even by God? When? What did you do about it? It is when things seem to be at their worst that Jesus carries us through. Staying in constant communication with him will not only help you bear the pain but also allow you to avoid future problems.

{ Faith }

Dearest Ann Marie,

I have had better days. My human frailty showed up yesterday, and I truly am sorry. With Nonno [Italian for grandpa] Giulio's illness and Nonno Alberto approaching one month in the hospital, and my own personal back pain and absentmindedness, I sometimes get frustrated. You saw me at my worst. Pray for me and the nonnos.

I am sorry for overreacting. I hope you forgive me. Pray hard, study hard, work hard, and love hard.

Love, Dad

When have you offended or hurt someone? Did you offer an apology? When have others offended or hurt you? Did you forgive them when they asked for forgiveness or did you carry a grudge? Remember: If you can't forgive others, how can you expect the Lord to forgive you?

Many relationships are strengthened after an apology is extended and accepted.

Think of people you have hurt in the past; send them a note or call them to say you are sorry. You'll feel one thousand pounds lighter.

{ Forgiveness }

Dearest Ann Marie,

I love you in so many ways for so many reasons. You know I am your number one fan.

I offer you this Lenten message: See Christ in everyone. Give of your time and talent to those who need it and would appreciate it most. Seek each day to make someone happy. A smile or "how are you today?" may be all that is required.

Love, Dad

Are you sharing your God-given gifts? Remember, God gave them to you to share with others. How can you be more active in your community, your school, your church?

Dearest Ann Marie,

What a great way to start the season of Lent. I am happy to see you understand that sacrifice is only a small part of the Lenten process, and that forgiveness, compassion, and charity are equally important.

You inspire us all by your example.

Love, Dad

How are you growing in your ability to forgive others? How are you becoming more patient and compassionate? Ask the Lord for help in forgiving. No one does it better.

{ Forgiveness }

Dearest Ann Marie,

Nonno Alberto [he passed away on
Valentine's Day 1999] must be very
pleased with us. He is more in our minds
than ever before. Maybe because he can
hear us now! [Nonno was nearly deaf his
last few years.]

We must remember, not only is he no
longer in pain, he is far happier than
any of us could imagine.

Have a wonderful time with the Al's Gals
crew at B. T.'s sweet sixteen. Give her
my love and best wishes.

Love, Dad

When have you experienced the loss of a loved one? What did you do to deal with this loss? The best way to remember a person you have lost is to live in his or her honor.

Has someone you know suffered a recent loss? If so, give your presence to them in this time of need.

{ **Loss** }

Dearest Ann Marie,

Remember to think about Nonno and smile today for him; he may be watching you from heaven. You can be sure he will smile, too.

Remember to love unconditionally with all your heart. . . . We never know the day or the hour when we will be called to justify our life.

In Dad's absence,
Love, Mom

What did you do today that would put a smile on the face of someone looking down on you? Be prepared—live each day as if the Lord was looking to catch you doing something *right*.

{ **Character, Loss** }

Dearest Ann Marie,

The Lord tells us that acts of forgiveness and sacrifice open our hearts to his love and our souls to his graces. The Lord instructs us to see him in everyone and therefore treat others accordingly. It's a lesson you have learned well. You demonstrate it every day and lead others by your good example. Nonno and I are so proud of you.

Brooklyn, here we come.
Be SMART!

Love, Dad

When have you judged others based on their outward appearance or their station in life? When have you treated others as if you saw Jesus present in them? If you can't judge a book by its cover, how can you judge a person by his "cover"?

_____

_____

_____

_____

_____

_____

_____

_____

_____

_____

_____

_____

_____

_____

_____

_____

{ Forgiveness }

Dearest Ann Marie,

I look forward to our daddy/daughter trip with great anticipation. As much fun as it will be, we must be prepared for love and concern disguised as criticism and/or cynicism. Listen and maintain your cool regardless of the circumstances. Always be respectful.

Let's agree to enjoy our family and each other on this hectic trip.

Love, Dad

Be really, really SMART!

When have your parents criticized you for something that you did or a decision that you made? How did it make you feel? Sometimes parents and well-meaning adults criticize the decisions or the choices you make. They do so not just because you erred, but more so because they love you and want to accentuate the mistake you made so that you will realize the magnitude of your error and will avoid making the same mistake again in the future. Sometimes the best response to criticism is to ask how you should have handled the situation. You will not only defuse the situation but may also achieve immediate reconciliation.

{ Failure }

Dearest Ann Marie,

You can accomplish more with God in an hour than you can in a lifetime without him.

Remain God-centered and, though life's trials and tribulations may not get easier, you will grow stronger, particularly if you ask the Lord to help you. Remember, ask and you shall receive.

So pray for the strength to deal with life's adversities, for therein lies the miracle.

Love, Dad

Do you remember to **Walk With Jesus Daily?** How do you involve him in your decision making and activities? When have you asked for his help? He never tires of hearing from you. He is available 24/7.

{ Faith, Prayer }

Dearest Ann Marie,

Life is a gift; live it with gusto every day. Don't worry about the future because most of what we worry about never occurs. If it does, however, then you worry twice about the same thing, don't you? So be happy just like the song says.

It only takes a few muscles to smile, but many to frown. Why not avoid muscle strain and smile? An old adage says, "A smile costs nothing but gives so much." Enjoy the reaction of those at whom you smile. Remember, happy people live longer and happier lives.

Love, Dad

What are you worried about right now? Is it something that has happened, or are you worrying about something that may never happen? Do you walk around with a frown on your face all day long? Why? Try to smile as often as you can. Many good things can happen. For instance, you may make someone's day, people may treat you better, you may feel better about yourself, and people may think you know something about them. Go ahead: Smile and have some fun watching how others respond.

{ Stress }

Dearest Ann Marie,

[Announcer] ". . . and the winner of the 'Best Daughter Any Dad Could Ever Hope For' award is Ann Marie. Ann Marie has previously received an award for the leading role in the family sitcom <u>Moving on to the East Coast,</u> (with apologies to <u>The Jeffersons</u>)." [Ann Marie's note: It had been my idea for us to consider moving back east.]

Ann Marie, you just won the ultimate award: a father's undying love. Now what are you going to do?

Love, Dad, a.k.a. the Director

When have you spent time with your family recently just enjoying them for who they are? Do you spend as much time with your family as you should? If not, what can you do to improve this situation? Before you know it, college, your career, marriage, and your own family will dominate your time, so please spend time enjoying your family now.

{ Family }

Dearest Ann Marie,

Thank you for a wonderful weekend in Brooklyn. It was very enjoyable and productive, wasn't it? You were the perfect young lady, bringing joy to Nonna Rosa, Nonno Giulio, and Nonna Grazia.

I will always treasure our times together. Certainly, these last few months have taught us, if nothing else, that life is precious, yet fleeting. We must take full advantage of the time given to us by touching as many lives as we can.

Memories are forever, so make them as special as you possibly can.

Love, Dad

hat are your favorite memories of your grandparents? What are your favorite memories of your whole family together?

If you are having trouble figuring out how to involve yourself with your family, try by showing them this book and reading a few of the selections on family together. It might lead to another great memory.

{ Family }

Dearest Ann Marie,

When you live with purpose and maintain a positive attitude, life is wonderful. It is God's wish, after all, that we be "joyful people." Sure, there will be the occasional setback or obstacle in our lives; but, regardless, we are to remain hopeful and joyful.

The positive outlook you have is contagious. Everyone around you appreciates it.

You make me proud.

Love, Dad

What setback or obstacle have you faced recently? How did you handle it? Have you made this connection yet: A positive attitude and a smile lead to a happier and more productive life? Try it—the results might surprise you.

{ Attitude }

Dearest Ann Marie,

When athletes are about to retire, they seem to be able to draw on their experience and whatever reserves they have left so as to go out in a burst of glory.

Think of applying this concept to your life these last few months in Agoura. [Ann Marie's note: We were a few months away from moving to the East Coast.]

Love, Dad

Think about a time when you were almost done with a project, performance, or event into which you had put a lot of time and effort. How did you feel? Were you excited, or did you feel a sense of loss? As you neared the end of this task, did you begin to lose interest in it? Did you find it hard to finish this project because circumstances weren't exactly as you would have liked them to be? Completing a project can often leave us with a multitude of feelings, especially if everything has not worked out like we hoped it would. Remember, however, that if everything always lined up exactly the way you would like, you would never gain experience.

{ Attitude }

Dearest Ann Marie,

Start and live each day as if it were your last day on Earth.

Every new day is a new beginning. Begin and end it joyfully. Count all your blessings, even those you cannot see.

Consider each day as the beginning of the rest of your life.

How do you choose to live out that life?

Love, Dad

id you live today to its fullest? What can you do tomorrow to make full use of your talents and skills? If you are not happy with your life, start a new one today!

{ **Attitude, Choices** }

Dearest Ann Marie,

Life is like a card game. You never know what cards you will be dealt. All you can do is play them the best you can.

In other words, we cannot choose the circumstances of our lives, but we can choose our attitude toward those circumstances.

Be SMART!

Love, Dad

What cards have you been dealt? Have you played them well? Have you made necessary adjustments in your life?

{ Attitude }

Dearest Ann Marie,

Live life well by "doing." Joy is in the doing. You have so much talent; use it and make yourself and others happy.

When there are setbacks and life looks gloomy, continue the "race." Look forward, forge ahead, trust your instincts, and never look back.

Seize the day.

Love always, Dad

When do you feel like you don't know what you are doing? When do you not know what to do next? Have you ever just crossed your fingers and moved ahead, even though you did not know in what direction to go? Sometimes you must eliminate your "safety nets" and be bold. Sometimes moving in any direction is better than standing still.

{ **Stewardship, Failure** }

Dearest Ann Marie,

St. Francis said: "Teach others the Gospel, and, if necessary, use words." What he meant was simply that our actions speak louder than words.

Our actions then become part of our character. Despite what the "spin meisters" say, character matters. We need to be honest and loyal, and we must have integrity.

To paraphrase a quote I once heard: "Anyone who thinks he can rise to the top and stay there without the qualities of honesty, loyalty, and integrity is dumb."

Love, Dad

hat do your actions say about you? Do others listen to what you say without words? Long after you are gone, your character is what people will remember most about you. How do you choose to be remembered?

{ Character }

Dearest Ann Marie,

A follow-up on character . . . character defines our life on Earth long after we are gone.

I read an interesting brochure about womanhood recently. Some of the points I remember were: A real woman is moral, modest, strong in faith, prayerful, and she cherishes her femininity.

That's all I recall, but that is enough to confirm you are a "real woman."

Love, Dad

n what ways are you moral, modest, strong in faith, and prayerful, and how do you cherish your femininity? Are you a "real woman," or does peer pressure or society's sometimes warped sense of values define you?

Ahem! The same goes for "real men."

{ Character }

Dearest Ann Marie,

Gale Sayers, a former football great, titled his autobiography I Am Third.

He meant God is first in his life, family and friends are second, and he is third.

Maintaining strong and positive relationships is an integral part of physical and spiritual happiness. I, for one, am happiest when I have a great relationship with the Lord, with Mom, with you and Anthony, as well as with myself.

Love, Dad

Are you first, second, or third in your life? Who is first? Who is second? Remember, Jesus said, "The last shall be first, and the first shall be last" (Matthew 20:16).

{ **Faith, Family, Friendship** }

Dearest Ann Marie,

Remember the moral of <u>The Pearl</u>:
Though we can never order our lives
(like a Hollywood script), we can put
order into our lives, regardless of
the circumstances.

When circumstances are unfavorable,
remember the lesson of "Footprints":
It's when life's burdens seem unbearable
that the Lord carries us.

Love, Dad

What seems unbearable in your life? What can you do to put order into your life? If you don't have a copy of "Footprints," do yourself a great service and get a copy from a local card store or off the Internet. Read it and meditate on its lesson. It's no longer than a lunch bag note.

{ **Attitude, Stress** }

Dearest Ann Marie,

"Do all the good you can, by as many means as you can, in as many places as you can, to as many people as you can, for as long as you can." Beautiful isn't it? It's an excerpt from a poem entitled "An Angel Says."

Love, Dad

How are you doing all the good that you can? What else can you do? You can summarize the line from "An Angel Says" in three words: Make today great. Write this line of poetry down and post it prominently on your bathroom mirror, your car dashboard, your locker, your night table, or some other location where you will see it every day.

{ Stewardship }

Dearest Ann Marie,

"I could have, I should have, but I didn't" are the sorriest of words.

You can only experience this life once. It is not a rehearsal. There are no "retakes." Experience all the good life has to offer, from the birds chirping to opening a present. For that matter, every day is a "present"! Open it up and you may find wonderful surprises.

Love, Dad

hen have you said those sorry words? What things could you and should you have done, but you didn't? Do you regret not taking action? Resolve to take advantage of opportunity when it comes your way. Be bold.

{ **Choices, Attitude** }

Dearest Ann Marie,

A quick follow-up to yesterday's theme—living life to the fullest: Live your life without regrets. The only caveat is to never let anything you do detour you from the "Staircase to Heaven."

Love, Dad

What have you done that you regret? What did you not do that you regret? Why do you have these regrets? Living life without regrets is easier than you think. First, you must always make your best effort. Anything worth doing is worth doing well.

{ **Choices, Attitude** }

Dearest Ann Marie,

Life is a series of events. The key is recognizing them. Each event offers us opportunities and challenges. Always confront opportunities and challenges with all the gusto you can muster because the opportunity may never cross your path again.

A great analogy comes to us from the Jewish Theological Seminary of America: "A human life is like a single letter in the alphabet. It can be meaningless. Or it can be a part of a great meaning."

Love, Dad

What opportunities and challenges have you accepted and met head on? What opportunities have you let slip away from you? Do you feel your life is meaningless or part of a great meaning? If you want to add meaning to your life, start out by doing little things great. Then move on from there.

{ Choices }

Dearest Ann Marie,

Contentment makes the rich feel poor, while it makes the poor feel rich. This is simply another way to express one of my favorite sayings: "Happiness is not having what you want; but rather, happiness is wanting what you have."

Love, Dad

Be SMART!

Are you happy? Why or why not? Do you want what you have, or are you always trying to have what you want? What is it you treasure?

Society may measure people's success by how much they own, but God doesn't, nor should you. Jesus tells us in one of his parables the story of a rich farmer who tore down his barn to build a larger one to store his produce, which he thought would sustain him for life. He was right: He died that night.

{ Happiness }

Dearest Ann Marie,

The only person home every time you call is the Lord, and it's a toll-free call from anywhere you find yourself. The Lord uses ancient (not state-of-the-art) wireless technology, so there is never any excuse not to call on him and chat.

Love, Dad

When something goes badly in your life, who is the first person you call on your cell phone or talk to? How about when something goes well? How often do you call God first? Maybe you should try it. His number is 1-800-PRAYNOW.

{ Prayer }

Dearest Ann Marie

Like everyone else, you will experience times when, despite your best efforts, you will fail. Most successful persons—from biblical characters to modern-day business, political, and sports icons—have failed several times before achieving success.

Regard failure as the "road to success," and you won't dwell on defeat, but rather appreciate the fact that you now know what pitfall(s) to avoid.

The rest of your life starts today. Be bold. Be SMART!

Love, Dad

What is your greatest failure? What have you failed at the most? No one can be great without first being a beginner—and that usually means "bad"— at something. Success is an earned reward for perseverance.

Dearest Ann Marie,

Last night was the culmination of ten years of religious education. Mom and I are so proud of you. You have balanced your life so well. Though we feel we laid a strong foundation, ultimately, it was you who chose to follow the right path and apply the Golden Rule.

Go forth in peace. Continue to love and serve God by loving and serving others.

Love, Dad

When have you asked yourself "How does this class apply to me?" or "How will this class help me in my adult life?" Though you may ask these questions about some classes at school, religious education is something you can use throughout your life.

{ Faith }

Dearest Ann Marie,

A 9-Step program, adapted from several sources, to share with Al's Gals:

1. See the glass as half full.
2. Maintain your values.
3. Be generous with your time, talent, and treasure.
4. Be compassionate.
5. Have a sense of humor.
6. See the good in others.
7. Be humble.
8. Be confident.
9. Be faithful.

Love, Dad

. . . and of course, be SMART!

How many of the items on this list are you applying to your life? Which are easy for you? Which cause you trouble. Use this checklist as your daily guide. Chart your progress; you'll be amazed at how you grow!

{ **Character, Choices** }

Dearest Ann Marie,

Life is not a rehearsal, it is the real thing. Live it with gusto because anything worth doing is worth doing well. Seize the day.

Love, Dad

When you spent a lot of time practicing for a performance or sporting event, how was the practice different from the actual event? Which was easier? Which was more rewarding?

Has it sunk in yet? Live life to the fullest by doing your "bestest" in everything you do.

{ Choices, Attitude }

Dearest Ann Marie,

You have heard me say countless times to maintain a positive attitude. Well, lately you have allowed someone else's problem to get you down. You cannot adopt another's problem; it helps neither you nor the other person.

Be empathetic and, if appropriate, offer advice and counsel, but never take ownership of the problem. Be SMART!

Love, Dad

When have you made a friend's problem your own? Were you able to help your friend by doing so, or did you just hurt yourself? Do you know the difference between having empathy for a friend and taking responsibility for her difficulties? In order to grow, sometimes friends have to face their own difficulties and own them.

{ Friendship }

Dearest Ann Marie,

Fear (false evidence appearing real) is a human frailty. This prayer is an excellent source of courage:

Deliver me Lord,

* From the fear of being humiliated,
* From the fear of being despised,
* From the fear of being left behind,
* From the fear of being wronged,
* From the fear of failure.

It is a wonderful prayer of humility, a virtue so absent today.

Love, Dad

hat scares you most? Why? Do you confront your fears, or do you let them linger? Which action—or inaction—do you think is the better choice?

Dearest Ann Marie,

You know how often the "little things" get us down. Remember, there is some good in every bad experience.

Disappointment, like friends who hurt us, tests the limits of our faith. You are mature enough not to let the weakness and/or insincerity of others change your outlook on life or your life's mission.

Love, Dad

What little things tend to get you down? When you experience a "minor" disappointment or setback, do you overreact, or do you just shrug your shoulders and acknowledge a new lesson learned?

Remember WWJD.

{ Failure }

Dearest Ann Marie,

Along with your silent daily prayers, recite aloud positive affirmations. This is the one I have been using for years. I don't even remember where I had read it:

1. I am divinely inspired.
2. Every day, in every way, I am getting better and better.
3. I am a good and happy person.

Love, Dad

Do you have any prayers or affirmations that you pray or say each day? Reciting affirmations aloud can help you hear the true meaning of the words. Find an affirmation, prayer, or poem that has meaning for you, and recite it every day. The effect of doing so will surprise you.

{ Prayer }

Dearest Ann Marie,

I recently read a brochure that was obviously created for teenagers struggling with the pressures of today's society.

The key points I remember are challenging and morally correct:

1. Do what is right, even when it's difficult.
2. Give yourself only to the special person you marry.
3. Respect all life, especially the unborn and the elderly.
4. Don't ever quit; if you fail, try again.

Love, Dad

Take a good look at this list. Do you have trouble doing anything on this list? If so, why? This is another list to post prominently and read often.

Dearest Ann Marie,

Every day you give Mom and me another reason to be proud of you.

Each time you give of yourself, God is giving you more of himself.

If it is true that actions speak louder than words, then you are truly shouting.

Keep it up, darling daughter.

Love, Dad

What have you done lately to make your parents and family proud of you? Have they noticed your positive actions and commented on them? Even if they haven't said anything to you directly, *their* actions may be telling you how proud they are.

{ Stewardship }

Dearest Ann Marie,

Jiminy Cricket said: "Let your conscience be your guide." Always make moral decisions, even when they are difficult to choose. If in doubt, seek advice and counsel; avoid making hasty decisions or making no decision at all, which is even worse. You can always rely on WWJD (What Would Jesus Do).

Every decision you make has an impact on your life and on the lives of others, so choose wisely. In small or big decisions, be SMART!

Love,
Dad

How do you make decisions when you are faced with a moral crisis? Do you follow your conscience or follow the crowd? Hard choices, when made wisely, will often make your life easier.

{ Choices }

Dearest Ann Marie,

Thank you for acknowledging me. I will always be there for you, my precious child. Even though someday you will marry and have your own family and home, I will never be more than a phone call away.

I want to spend as much time with you as possible.

Love, your number one fan,
Dad

Do you acknowledge all your parents do for you? When was the last time you thanked them for all the positive contributions they make to your life? Though parents are adults, they still need to know that they are appreciated. If you don't know what to say, start with, "I love you," especially if it's been a while since you last said it.

{ Family }

Dearest Ann Marie,

Science has proven that cheerful people live healthier and longer lives. Fortunately, cheerfulness is contagious. Spread the epidemic every day.

Cheerful people, by nature, have a positive attitude and outlook on life. Let the world know you're happy. Your smile is like a billboard. Advertise the beauty of life with your smile. It costs you nothing, yet it gives others so much. Also, it is very difficult to be sad when you're smiling.

Love, Dad

re you a cheerful person? What are you doing to spread the epidemic? If you have doubts about whether your attitude makes a difference, try it. Be cheerful to everyone you meet tomorrow morning. What can it hurt?

Dearest Ann Marie,

Give your friends and teachers a gift this week, one for each day of the week.

1. charity
2. an open ear
3. forgiveness
4. gratitude
5. a good example
6. service
7. loyalty

Remember, giving is better than receiving.

Love, Dad

Try this out in your life. Write down the name of a person to whom you can give each gift on the list. For a week, give one of the gifts every day. Keep a record of what happened. Did you make a difference in anyone's life? How?

Dearest Ann Marie,

Sometimes, Honey, it is better, or even necessary, to be the heart of the matter rather than the head. Sometimes a leader or a veteran has to step aside so others can have the opportunity to grow.

I am always your number one fan and your genie rolled into one. "You ain't ever had a friend like me."

Love, Dad

Are you a leader in your group or a follower? Do you jealously guard your social position among your peer group? Do you make the decisions for your group, or do you follow someone else's decisions? Is it time to let someone else lead for a change so that she can grow, or is it time for you to grow?

{ **Friendship, Character** }

Dearest Ann Marie,

Sometimes talent alone isn't sufficient enough to succeed. Lasting success requires patience, integrity, and the ability to hurdle obstacles.

President Calvin Coolidge put it this way: "Persistence and determination alone are omnipotent."

Love, Dad

When have you shown your persistence? If success was easy, then everyone could be successful, rendering the term meaningless.

Success is never easy.

Dearest Ann Marie,

I loved you since before you were born, and that love continues to grow daily—most recently, as a result of your concern and love for your grandparents.

You are a wonderful person, willing to do the right thing despite the hardships you will endure. That is certainly Christ-like.

Love, Dad

How have your parents shown you unconditional love? It can be hard to understand how a parent can love you more when you show what a loving and caring person you are becoming, but that is usually what happens. As your parents watch you grow, you amaze them, and their love for you grows.

{ Choices }

Dearest Ann Marie,

<u>Life Is Beautiful</u> is not only the title of a wonderful film but also a reality. A reality we can each make with:

* a positive attitude
* a sense of self-worth
* adherence to the Golden Rule
* believing that happiness is wanting what you already have

Love, Dad

Is your life beautiful? Do you have the four characteristics on the list that make it beautiful?

If you need convincing that life is beautiful, that goodness can be found in the worst of times, rent the movie.

{ Attitude, Happiness }

Dearest Ann Marie,

More ways to be a happy teenager:

* Know, love, and serve God by loving
  and serving others.
* Set high standards for yourself and
  reach for the "impossible star."
* Be a "pack rat" and do things as
  a group, enjoying the company of
  Al's Gals.

Love, Dad

Are you doing all three things on this list? These are all choices you can make to create a happier and more fulfilling life. Try these three ways to be happy if you haven't already. Hint: Does the first one seem difficult? Amazingly enough, that one makes the others easy.

Dearest Ann Marie,

Friendship is a gift to give and a gift to receive. It is a priceless gift never to be taken for granted.

Be generous with your gift, but be equally prudent about to whom you choose to gift it, and equally wise about from whom you accept it.

Love, Dad

Have you ever thought of your friendship as a gift? To whom would you like to give it? From whom would you accept it? Give some thought to who your friends are, and maybe even who they should be.

{ Friendship }

Dearest Ann Marie,

Things often happen to us unexpectedly.

That is why we need to always be prepared, as there are no guarantees in life. Unfortunately, we get caught up in our daily lives, oblivious to our surroundings. At the same time, we often get distracted from what really matters.

Sounds like a good time to be reminded of the Boy Scout motto: "Be prepared." Remember, too, that Jesus told us, "We know not the day, nor the hour."

Love, Dad

You probably prepared well for your last vacation, your driver's permit, driver's test, and your last exam. Shouldn't you also "prepare" well for your soul? Play hard, work hard, live hard, and pray hard. How much preparation have you made for your faith exam, your final vacation?

{ Attitude }

Dearest Ann Marie,

Think about Nonno Alberto today. Say a prayer for him and give him a big smile. He is watching you from heaven and will smile back to you.

Remember to love unconditionally with all your heart. See Christ in everyone. Nonno reminds us that we never know when we will be called to justify our life.

In Dad's absence,

Love, Mom

Loss often reminds us to think about how we are living our lives. Do you remember to love unconditionally with all your heart? Do you remember, even during conflicts with others, that the spirit of Christ Jesus, our Lord, is in everyone?

{ **Loss** }

Dearest Ann Marie,

I have heard it said you can accomplish more with God in one hour than you can in a lifetime without Him.

Always remain God-centered. Though life's trials and tribulations may not disappear, or even lessen, you will grow stronger. Remember, during your most difficult times, don't pray your troubles should all go away. Pray for wisdom and the strength to deal with your problem(s).

In this way you become the "miracle."

Love, Dad

How do you deal with difficult times? What actions do you take? Trouble in your life can often be just the encouragement you needed to stop and pray. Remember, prayer can be short and quick, like repeating Jesus' name. If you talked to the Lord a few minutes every hour, before you know it the time would add up to an hour. Then, who knows what you might accomplish!

{ **Prayer** }

Dearest Ann Marie,

Just another reminder how blessed you are with talent. Talent, unlike a natural resource, diminishes without use.

I urge you to share your singing and dancing artistry, if not for profit, for charity, as you have done on occasion.

You have the time and talent to touch so many lives. I don't want you to ever look back and think or say those horrible words: "I could have, I should have, but I didn't."

Love, Dad

Have you discovered your talent yet? Is it one of the arts, is it the ability to mentor children, is it reading aloud to a senior, or something else? What are you doing when you feel most alive? Whatever your talent is, the more you use it, the stronger it gets.

{ Stewardship }

Dearest Ann Marie,

Whether we remain in California or move back east to Brooklyn or New Jersey, we will be together and support each other. Whatever we do, we will do it together.

Isn't that what family is all about?

Love, Dad

ow supportive are you of your family? My friend, Mary Ellen, once wrote me an e-mail, in which she said, "We can often judge how good our relationship with God is by how good our relationships are with those we are closest to." How are your relationships with your family and closest friends? Is there any way to make them stronger?

{ **Family** }

Dearest Ann Marie,

Whatever you decide to do these last few weeks in Agoura—or for that matter for the rest of your life—do it with gusto. As I have told you before, it doesn't matter if the task is menial or great, it matters that you do it great.

Remember the example of Helen Keller, who endeavored to do great things by doing all things great.

Love, Dad

re you great? Do you do anything great? In what do you want to be great? If you are still doubtful of your ability to be great, Helen Keller's words should become your hallmark.

{ **Attitude, Choices** }

Dearest Ann Marie,

I know I frequently speak and write to you and Al's Gals about the importance of character. The reason I do is because character is how others perceive and judge us.

Many sports stars, entertainers, businessmen, and political leaders out there, by their words and actions, would have you believe character is irrelevant. I assure you it is most relevant.

Along with honesty and integrity, character will distinguish you from the crowd. Dare to stand a cut above the crowd.

Love, Dad

ow is your character relevant in your life? Do you feel that it distinguishes you from the crowd? Are you standing *tall* and *above* the crowd yet? If you aren't, why not?

_____

_____

_____

_____

_____

_____

_____

_____

_____

_____

_____

_____

_____

_____

_____

_____

_____

{ **Character** }

Dearest Ann Marie,

When we have a healthy self-esteem, constructive criticism is appreciated. Too often, however, we let our pride get in the way and we view constructive criticism as its ugly cousin—criticism.

The difference in the two is that while constructive criticism is positive, criticism is negative and meant to bring others down. You will know the difference by who offers it to you and in how the message is delivered.

Love, Dad

What is the difference between constructive criticism and plain criticism? Do you know it when you hear it? Accept constructive criticism in the spirit with which it is intended. On the other hand, if you feel criticized unfairly, just look the person straight in the eye and say, "Thank you," nothing more. Keep looking at the person squarely in the eye (you may perspire on this one), and observe the effect you have. Remember, silence is golden. Be stoic; don't laugh.

{ Failure }

Dearest Ann Marie,

Go out in style!

The next chapter begins. . . .

Make it great with an even higher attitude.

Love, Dad

Is anything in your life at an ending point? What do you plan to do now? When something in our life ends, it is a good time to take a look at our lives and how we want to proceed. New beginnings bring new opportunities.

{ Attitude }

Dearest Ann Marie,

Today is your last day of school here in Agoura. Your composure has been incredible. You inspire me with your unselfishness and self-sacrifice.

I am so glad God blessed me with you.

Cherish every moment with your friends these last few weeks in California. Remember your friends will only be a phone call, or an e-mail, or an Instant Message away.

They say absence makes the heart grow fonder; therefore, whenever we visit our friends here in Agoura, our time together will be great.

I have thoroughly enjoyed writing these notes for the girls through you. I hope you have enjoyed reading and sharing them as much as I have enjoyed writing them.

Love always and forever,
Your number one fan . . . Dad

You are SMART!

Similarly, we have enjoyed sharing these simple, thought-provoking messages of love and advice with you, the reader. We hope that the commentary has been useful to you and that you took the time to journal your thoughts. We hope the book has helped you communicate better, energized you to live life with gusto and with purpose, and increased your faith in God, who makes all things possible.

We urge you to reread the notes often. You may want to highlight the notes most relevant to you for easy reference. We also would like to remind you, if you haven't already done so, to prominently post your favorite affirmations, prayers, and goals. Remember to be bold, and start immediately without hesitation or reservation to improve your life. Your happiness is in your hands, and God wants to help.

Be SMART! . . .

And may God bless you and yours with abundant graces and joy.

—Ann Marie & Al Parisi

Epilogue
Ann Marie Parisi

Where are they today? At the time this edition goes to press, all of Al's Gals will be entering their senior year at their respective universities: Angela at Saint Mary's College in San Francisco; B. T. at the University of California, San Diego; Becky at Washington State University; Brynn at the University of California, Irvine; Erin at the Los Angeles School of Art; Jenny and Malia at California State University, Northridge; Julia at the University of San Francisco; Marissa at the University of California, Los Angeles; and myself at California Lutheran University in Thousand Oaks, California.

I am majoring in elementary-school education and hope to begin teaching next year in the Catholic parochial school system, preferably in my home parish of St. Jude the Apostle. The reason I chose to become a teacher is that several years ago, at my dad's and Mrs. Joan Nardone's (our Parish Director of Religious Education) constant urging, I started to teach religious education to first communion children. I did it to placate them more than anything, but, as it turned out, I fell in love with the children and enjoyed teaching them immensely. I still teach at St. Jude's Roman Catholic Church, and I also teach at the City of Agoura Hills after-school program. This is just one of the ways that Dad has influenced my life, but I would also like to give credit to my mom for all her support and encouragement. Mom and Dad are an effective team, as you have probably already surmised.

Epilogue

All of us begin our education at home. Our parents are our first teachers. I have been blessed with two outstanding parents who understood this responsibility. I am forever grateful.

Thank you, Mom and Dad.

Epilogue
Al Parisi

find things have not changed very much. My activities in and around the community are basically the same. However, I have made it clear to everyone that I am no longer Mr. Mom, but rather Chairman and CEO of Parisi Enterprises. I even announced it to the congregation of St. Jude's a few weeks ago when I was asked to speak on stewardship.

My health is basically fine, except for the damage caused by the brain tumor and radiation. I am still writing lunch bag notes. They are now addressed, however, exclusively to my son, Anthony. Anthony made certain in advance that, if I was going to write him notes, they had to be on a separate piece of paper and put *into* the lunch bag. Apparently, a sports jock can't be seen reading notes from his dad.

The joy of writing the lunch bag notes—or perhaps just lunch notes now—has not diminished. The feelings I experienced while writing them to Ann Marie are still there. I get great satisfaction when Anthony and I discuss the notes and their application in his life. As with Ann Marie and her friends (and now with you), I rarely miss an opportunity to motivate and encourage Anthony and his friends to make sound decisions in their lives, be of good character, communicate with their parents, and follow the Golden Rule.

P.S. Teenagers, I strongly urge you to share this book with your parents, especially if you have had trouble communicating with them. Parents, I urge you to affirm your children, inspire them to believe in themselves and to make sound choices in their lives. I urge you to write to your children, whether on their lunch bag or on a separate piece of paper dropped into the lunch bag or, perhaps, left on their pillow. If your child is away at school, write them frequently. The letter you write will have a greater impact than a phone call. As parents, we are challenged to protect and nurture our children, and some topics are better discussed in writing, primarily because we have more time to gather our thoughts.

Index of Themes

What Did You Think?

Teenagers, we would like to hear from you. Let us know how *Lunch Bag Notes* has affected you. Tell us which notes were the most meaningful to you and why. Send us your personal affirmations.

Parents, we would truly enjoy your sharing your thoughts as well. Are you writing lunch bag notes yourself, or have you developed another unique way to communicate with your kids? Do you have a favorite note that you've written and would like to share? If so, we would love to hear about it. We might even collect the best ones in a future anthology.

Please mail any correspondence to:

Ann Marie Parisi and Al Parisi
P.O. Box 1365
Agoura Hills, CA 91376